DarWrites: Writing Prompts

Darlene Reilley

DarWrites: Writing Prompts, Book 1

Read ~ Write ~ Play

Darlene Reilley

Works by Darlene Reilley

Books
1,001 Plot Ideas to Get You Started
DarWrites: Writing Prompts Book 1
Forbidden Timeline
Zombie Slayer

Short Stories
Bones and Stones
Day of the Dead
The Lady
The Legacy
Walk On
The Shovel

Poetry
American Girl
Mulder and Me
Poetry from the Heart: God, Guys, and the Rest of It
We the Explorers

Blog
DarWrites

Writing as Brianna Flannigan
The Pink Book of Romance

DarWrites: Writing Prompts, Book 1

Darlene Reilley

Roosevelt, Utah

ISBN-13: 978-1718611993

ISBN-10: 1718611994

Thank you to my DarWrites readers! I have learned so much in my journey to becoming a writer and I'm grateful for the opportunity to talk with you about writing and the writing life. My goal with DarWrites is to create a place where writers and readers can explore the world of books and learn about art, craft, and inspiration. I'm so grateful to my audience for sharing your time with me. You are awesome!

Special thanks to Chris Weigand and Stacey Oberlee for being fantastic writer buddies!

Write on.

Darlene

1. She is forced to walk between worlds
2. The seventh and perfect prayer saves them
3. What they wish they had said
4. At New Years, they wanted to look ahead to the possibilities
5. Looking back on his life, he regrets…
6. The man with cancer creates a Master Life List of things to do before he dies
7. The historian is forced to go on a long dangerous journey
8. She wants to stand out against the sea of women
9. The writer pitches her only novel at a conference
10. He offers her a simple, clear call to action
11. A catastrophe happens forcing one woman to use the bug out kit she thought she'd never have to use
12. After stepping off the world for the first time, explorers find a star portal
13. A traveler witnesses a ceremonial sacrifice
14. Travelers create a repository of technology
15. She spends a year in a cabin to write her novel
16. The man she promised to love forever drops her for his ex-girlfriend
17. His #1 life goal is to sell a million records
18. The depressed girl wants to wallow until her friend calls in reinforcements
19. If he decides to do it, he promises to win
20. She is full of moxie today
21. She creates a blog about ___________
22. The witch imbues the paper with the breath of her heart and sends it out to find her soulmate
23. Thank him for me
24. He must say what no one else could
25. She knows the trick of the trade that could win the account
26. The bestselling mystery writer creates a one-night-stand romance novel that turns out to be his best work ever
27. He tries to be worthy of her love, but can't get out of his own way
28. Every time she shaves her legs, something bad happens
29. She decides to quit school and go on a one-year hike
30. How can he make the next two years be a phenomenal learning experience

31. What are the crazy idiosyncrasies she wants to work on
32. The antagonist falls for the good woman who has a boyfriend and a dog
33. He opens his door to find a mermaid in the hallway
34. All she wants is one last chance
35. The vagabond with the six string on his back falls for the town's golden girl
36. She couldn't believe she made the call
37. A case of mistaken identity turns into a cat burglary
38. He dives off a cliff into an ocean, but lands in another universe
39. A translator with a talented tongue and a connection to a higher power overflows with ideas to help humanity
40. Reincarnated lovers reunite
41. The man with amnesia must reunite with his wife and children
42. He wants to rant, he wants to rave, but he can only cry because of his loss
43. Explain something your character learned years ago
44. Write bad poetry and level it up with craft
45. Explore the personality types she adopts for different jobs
46. A science teacher has trouble getting students to focus on a project
47. The person interrupts the superhero's transformation
48. Tectonic plates shift and they deal with the aftermath
49. He is stuck in the shallow end of life
50. The dentition falls for the dog walker
51. The gamer is addicted to their work
52. A cultural shockwave reverberates around the world
53. Create a fun lesson for children – bonus for illustrations
54. All he ever wanted is a tribe of his own
55. List the five things he wants most in the world
56. A child explores intelligent cities of the future
57. The dog wants to be near his friend and travels across the city to find the friend
58. The story starts with an unexpected journey
59. A moon-based dystopian story
60. Geek writing about geeks
61. List the five things he wants most of all

62. Pick a fresh point of view on a classic fairy tale
63. I wish I knew about ______
64. What matters most to them
65. He makes a huge promise to answer a big question and figures out how to deliver
66. Start with an amazing character and see where they lead you
67. Choose a setting that inspires you like Bali and go from there
68. Start with an idea like the paranormal and run with it
69. Use your dreams as novel fuel
70. An overheard conversation triggers action
71. Use your memories as novel fodder
72. The lover have a tryst
73. The undercover private investigator meets with her contact
74. An entrepreneur uncovers the competition's evil secret
75. Start with a comedic conversation
76. Write from the perspective of an inanimate object
77. A 7th child of a 7th child must contend with darkness and light
78. An unbeliever's childhood wishes come true
79. After an environmental disaster, humanity flees to the stars
80. Explore the reversal of poles
81. He walks away from his life
82. This is what he would kill for
83. She wins the $16 million dollar lotto
84. She places an ad to meet a bunch of smart, and almost, but not quite intimidating hikers
85. The fate of the world rests on a rock hound and what her marine uncle taught her
86. She runs away
87. Would they be willing to break him out of prison
88. A 4-million-year-old lake sealed in ice opens because of global warming
89. The storm of the century is about to hit
90. His confession stuns her
91. She infuriates him, and he inspires her
92. He says, "no worries," but his tone belies the look in his eyes
93. She was one of the smartest women of her time
94. The failed entrepreneur establishes a new enterprise
95. Her sister's life choices really confuse her

96. A five-person team explores the vastness of space and each other's idiosyncrasies
97. He dared her to love him
98. An out-of-work photographer moves to find a new career
99. He gets his best ideas in the shower
100. She writes a list to attract a companion
101. What would he do if aliens invaded Earth today
102. A depressed mechanic explores life in a small town
103. A veterinarian must contend with a werewolf infestation
104. He wanted to do this since he was a child
105. A shimmer of fairies accidentally travels across the vail into modern-day Australia
106. The bank accidentally gives her $100,000
107. His tribe welcomes him through a rite of passage
108. He becomes a wedding officiant
109. Write about the color that makes you happiest
110. Combine a favorite subject with a character that makes you angry and see what sparks fly
111. She signs up for a crash course that changes her life
112. The computer genius creates the first sentient artificial intelligence
113. Earthlings travel to go to Orion and find an ancient civilization
114. Teens playing an Oijia board meet a troubled spirit
115. The caregiver burns out
116. The witch accidentally turns her audience into horses
117. It was the biggest wardrobe failure of her life
118. He spends half his life waiting for computers to load
119. A volunteer encounters a mischievous paranormal entity
120. The corporate tycoon volunteers to feed otters at the zoo
121. The gamer is sucked into the video game
122. The virtual assistant discovers her boss is a hitman
123. He wakes up with a tattoo and a new dog who speaks to him
124. He must deal with a toxic work relationship
125. To him, family just means shared blood

126.	The divorced couple finds mutual respect, love, and support
127.	It is the end of verbal warfare among two clans
128.	Astronauts work on a space station
129.	He builds ships but never has sailed the sea
130.	Friends go on vacation during spring break
131.	Explore the heart's most secret desire
132.	Create a comedy about the best vacation destination spot no one visits
133.	She flies around the world to get a job, and finds this instead
134.	The redneck lawyer moves to the US Virgin Islands
135.	He creates a recipe for a new drink as big as whiskey
136.	Where do unfulfilled dreams go to die
137.	The sous chef creates deluxe dinners on the cheap
138.	The barista takes a job as a tutor to travel the world with his client
139.	An artist finds out that her creations have been stolen and mass produced
140.	He has his buddy create twenty questions to ask his potential wife
141.	A disillusioned monk leaves his monastery and finds his true self and calling
142.	The little girl who is bullied finds her voice and writes a play that shows exactly what it feels like to be bullied
143.	A woman who is horrible at cooking creates a masterpiece
144.	A dog travels through time and helps people
145.	A farmer finds a trove of ancient writings and treasure
146.	The troubled college student takes a train trip around the country to find herself and her future
147.	"I'm pregnant," she admits. He looked at her as if the kid would pop out any second. "Relax, hero, it's not due for two months."
148.	After watching a tv show, a creature from the show comes to life
149.	The librarian loves banned books

150.	An angel comes to earth with orders to help a person in crisis

151.	A relic hunter gives up the adventurous life for a house and settled life

152.	The firefighter saves his future wife

153.	A writer's assistant bot develops into a sentient intelligence

154.	The baker falls in love with a lactose intolerant person

155.	Her child died of a heart condition and dedicates her life to changing medicine

156.	The researcher and a doctor cure cancer

157.	A housebound woman finds out her neighbor's shocking secret

158.	A work-at-home mom decides to work at a café

159.	She moves to a coffee plantation because she adores the drink

160.	In the hunt for the perfect workout, a climber creates a new workout

161.	The masseuse saves an abandoned dog and the dog saves his life in return

162.	The painter on a deadline moves to a cabin in the woods

163.	A truck driver explores life on the road

164.	She revolutionizes the pet industry

165.	He decides to get a PhD in bioarchaeology

166.	A clerk creates a revolutionary new toy

167.	The soup company woos a woman for her great-grandmother's recipe

168.	The single father listens to his daughter and joins a club

169.	This designer creates a new fashion trend more popular than jeans

170.	Write about the matchmaker who brings people together is off her game

171.	The demon pushes people away

172.	He sits down for coffee at a table beside two working writers and can't believe the conversation

173.	He can travel to any time or place

174.	The long-distance backpacker returns to a changed world
175.	The hiker's perspective changes as they walk
176.	They leave their homeland to create a new culture because of persecution
177.	The reporter changes the lives of an indigenous population
178.	A newfound relationship is founded on a football bet
179.	Write about the passage of time
180.	The time management professional can't focus
181.	The hero is worse than the villain
182.	The bride is terrified of tying the knot
183.	She sells her deceased ex-husband's things and meets a stranger who claims one of the maps in her possession is a treasure map
184.	A pack of werewolves moves in down the street from your character
185.	Their goodbye is a second chance
186.	How he feels when he turns into a werewolf
187.	Write an immigration story from the perspective of a child
188.	A skeptic goes on an underground ghost tour of Seattle
189.	He creates a new evolution in entertainment bigger than tv and video games
190.	The wishing well was the center of the town from the beginning
191.	The research becomes afraid of their creation
192.	Transmogrification goes awry
193.	Nanotechnology leaps into humanity
194.	The psychic is caught in an astral projection
195.	The inventor creates a new fuel source
196.	A hive mind explores the future of humanity
197.	We evolve into light beings
198.	An intellectual bad ass and a tough fighter battle evil
199.	Magic and technology merge
200.	Write about freedom's blade
201.	She finds out about her mother's secret past after her funeral

202.	She is expected to marry, but defies her culture's command
203.	The man loves his family more than anything must save them from invaders
204.	Write a dystopian story from the perspective of a defiant teenager
205.	A child wakes up psychic and can now see dead people
206.	She reboots her life
207.	They create a new religion
208.	A botanist explores six ways to save the world's crops
209.	Everything a person needs for life is embedded in a microchip
210.	She studies natural history against her father's wishes
211.	Write a list of 39 perfect things
212.	The wounded soldier saves a golden retriever and falls for the veterinarian
213.	He leads from behind for a reason
214.	She loved him but couldn't live with him
215.	The mechanic who lived in the same town his whole life
216.	The astrophysicist decides to study medicine
217.	He takes up the law
218.	Write about a relic hunter's misadventures
219.	He demands a cost she didn't expect
220.	They must choose between diamonds or magic
221.	A magician reunites a world split into reality and magic by an evil sorcerous
222.	While on vacation, a woman's best friend mails letters she wrote to her ex-husband who seeks her out to rekindle their relationship
223.	She is pulled through a portal in time to another dimension
224.	The country singer retires to take care of her family
225.	The popular tv star falls for a fan
226.	Write about the legend of Earth
227.	A scientist thinks of love as an incurable disease

228.	She sells everything she owns and move to an island to teach
229.	Write about a 12-year-old's Christmas list
230.	Johnny doesn't want anyone to know his real name
231.	She always drives ten miles under the speed limit
232.	Willow's mother isn't curious enough
233.	Mary prays the rosary every morning and twice on Tuesday because of this
234.	She only notices things that are pink
235.	She walks on sunshine
236.	He needs a sword to cut through her shield
237.	The introvert must contend with an extroverted roommate
238.	The extrovert is trapped in a snowstorm with introverts
239.	She never wakes before 1 PM
240.	He runs five miles per day
241.	The desert feels like home to him
242.	Combine the end of common sense and an identity shift
243.	It is a test of faith
244.	In the Book of Answers everything is written
245.	A boat captain contends with distractions
246.	Write about the accidental vegan
247.	A tall tattooed and dangerous man knocks on the door
248.	The girl walks into a tea room at Christmas time
249.	A knitter is hired to host a television show about crafts
250.	The reluctant yoga teacher moves on after a breakup
251.	Write about an artic lake and the critters found within
252.	After a break, a student enrolls in summer school to graduate on time
253.	The couple survives a biohazard and strengthens their relationship
254.	Lost hikers work together to find their way out of the wilderness
255.	An earthquake uncovers an underwater forest
256.	The superhero does this on Sunday mornings

257. The studio photographer is famous for discovering her client's true identity
258. A tomboy southern belle studies abroad
259. Write about a strategic relocation
260. There are strange disappearances from national parks
261. An empath has to learn how to tune her abilities
262. The gun can kill anything—even gods
263. The novice gets lost while soul searching in the woods
264. Three sisters reunite to solve a family mystery
265. The child is the sole survivor of a pirate attack
266. At the wedding of the century, a bride falls for someone else
267. After a hurricane, he rebuilds his life from scratch
268. The powerful woman runs a company
269. The shopper decides to only order from home and have things delivered
270. She explores friendship and love in the deep south
271. A soldier falls for a barmaid
272. The daughter of a famous chef holds cooking classes
273. He is set to wage war on the world
274. Write about the gift of sisterhood/brotherhood
275. The single mom decides to make money from home
276. A man moves to Florida to recover after a major loss
277. After a major storm, shipwrecked survivors survive on a tropical island
278. He was told not to tempt fate, but can't help it
279. A couple adopt orphaned twins
280. She moves off the grid and create a homestead from scratch
281. A consultant is hired to protect an asset in a foreign land
282. Write about the change of power structure in society
283. She stole another woman's idea
284. He decides to read every self-help book and find his true love
285. A woman gives up fairy tales meets her Prince Charming
286. She stops suffering in silence

287.	Triplet brothers fight for the future of their people
288.	He throws a house party for his girlfriend who only wants to knit
289.	What is the difference between being nomadic and being homeless
290.	His nightmares begin with a kiss
291.	The boy spoke of being born on a war-ravaged planet, but never left home
292.	Archaeologists discover a 7,000-year-old burial site
293.	Underwater explorers establish a colony under the sea
294.	A polyglot cannot connect with the person next to her
295.	A computer program plots to kill a scientist
296.	A scientific experiment based on benevolence goes awry
297.	A self-help guru has an identity crisis
298.	She writes an article which receives unwanted attention from aliens
299.	She falls in love with an Alien intergalactic special forces operative
300.	Two people meet and fall in love via Pinterest
301.	A couple joins Asgardia and are issued a special invitation
302.	The lost heir of Leonardo da Vinci must solve a problem his ancestor created
303.	He writes her name on the moon and ten thousand years later their ancestors return to tell their story
304.	She never saw snow until this moment
305.	Pictures just in from NASA telescopes show something unusual in space
306.	An academic sets out to solve one of the great questions of her time
307.	He manages the conflict between his siblings while falling in love
308.	After a party, two partygoers get into mischief
309.	She moves to Hawaii to become a teacher
310.	A hacker goes into a target's computer, but finds more than he's looking for – he stumbles into a murder-for-hire plot and the killer comes after him

311.   She wants to read all the must read books, but is distracted by a little black cat

312.   He applies for a job at a cruise line and is accepted

313.   He takes a job as an archivist but gets more than he bargained for when he meets the library's trolls

314.   She takes a job with FEMA to pay off her student loans

315.   He creates a portfolio of his work that blows away the completion

316.   The lecturer interrupts a crime

317.   A creative writer becomes a world-renowned travel photographer

318.   The expert job hunter finds a job for everyone except for herself

319.   He wishes her all the happiness in the world – and means it

320.   The curse rebounds on her

321.   She devotes every waking moment to her job hunt

322.   The caricature artist falls in love with a tramp

323.   She promises to never cry again and dedicate her life to _________

324.   He searches for his calling, but finds this instead

325.   After twenty years of traveling, an artist returns to her hometown

326.   The writer was called by his pen name so often, he doesn't respond to his own name anymore, but when he meets her, he falls hard and has to tell her that he isn't who she thinks he is

327.   She takes a job as a user experience manager and falls for one of the participants

328.   The farmer from Nebraska who lost everything in a fire starts over in Colorado

329.   The entrepreneur fails for the last time and returns to corporate life

330.   He moves across the country to take a job as a staff writer

331.   A carpenter/homesteader romances a teacher in Alaska

332.   A baker wins a trip to Spain and $25K

333.	They meet at an IKEA store between the linens and workspaces
334.	The real estate agent falls for the nomadic surfer
335.	She takes a job working as a Rent-a-friend
336.	It snows in paradise the day this happens
337.	The English major takes a temporary job to make ends meet and finds a rewarding career under unusual circumstances
338.	A bohemian embraces minimalism after sickness
339.	In a personal crisis, she becomes her own hero
340.	After breaking her foot, a woman must recover for a month
341.	A plague sweeps the land creating a zombie apocalypse
342.	Something about him is off, but she isn't sure what
343.	Persistence meets resistance and chaos ensues in one woman's life
344.	A man finds his true calling as a fisherman
345.	He falls in love with a novelist's words but she thinks he's a little strange
346.	A burned-out archivist opens a ski shop
347.	He writes a letter to his hero and has dinner with her
348.	A wayward waif falls for a karate instructor
349.	A researcher stumbles into a centuries-old mystery
350.	The traveling lecturer settles down to teach classics
351.	The bored muse comes to Earth to inspire someone with a new bestseller, but she is sick and things get wonky
352.	The AirBnB host rents to a mystery writer
353.	The visiting professor declared his intention to write a novel about her life – and becomes obsessed with his artist-muse
354.	The world traveling photographer settles down
355.	A retired soldier meets the love of his life while taking her class at a college
356.	He decides to hike the Pacific Coast Trail and within 48 hours heads out
357.	The romance writer falls for her cover model
358.	She takes a course entitled Mastering Your People Skills and it changes her life

359.	A novice writes a novel with the greatest villain in literature
360.	An orphan explores her history including skeletons best left buried
361.	A claims adjuster goes into a disaster area after a natural disaster and sees a complex case like an industrial site
362.	A civilization faces its destruction as one of its moons breaks orbit and plunges toward the planet
363.	I have to deactivate you
364.	She sees a circle of stones and realizes she isn't where she was supposed to be
365.	He enters a literary contest for the first time and wins the grand prize
366.	The visiting professor declares his intention to write a novel about an artist and becomes obsessed with his artist-muse
367.	A hockey player with an injury takes a year off to recuperate and helps coach a team of children
368.	She lost her mojo but takes extreme measures to regain her charisma
369.	While studying abroad, a student falls in love for the first time
370.	She never bought lotto tickets, but the total was so high, she decided to – and won
371.	A rare find discovered in Colorado sheds light on Spanish colonial history
372.	Hidden meanings found in ancient scrolls
373.	Aliens inspire writers on Earth to create a massive collection of data – and show themselves after it's published to world acclaim
374.	A one-dose universal vaccine is found that cures cancer
375.	Archaeologists discover ancient tombs beneath Bali volcanoes
376.	The quiet man falls for the librarian
377.	A reporter and a hockey player are snowed in a hotel
378.	Stranded in a desert, a crash victim must fight to survive
379.	She learns a language while exploring another culture

380.   The hiker studies physics for fun
381.   The social media specialist tries snorkeling for the first time
382.   Jane from Michigan plays an online game with a hitman
383.   An indigenous person gets a higher education to help his people
384.   She loves social media, but has to abstain
385.   Click-click-slaw-click-click-slaw
386.   An EM pulse weapon triggers a worldwide emergency
387.   The salon owner falls for a pair of gold sandals, but doesn't know about the genie that comes with the pair of shoes
388.   Don't judge me – I haven't seen it yet
389.   The private eye has puppy eyes and a cleft chin
390.   She pretends she is on a phone call, but listens to the conversation before her
391.   A man smarter than Einstein and artistic like da Vinci solves crimes
392.   They come in waves of tribes, smaller and smaller, until there are none left
393.   The farmers become immigrants heading to a new world
394.   Aliens live among earthlings and are forced to blend
395.   A man goes on vacation for the first time and aliens invade
396.   A woman begins an around-the-world boating trip
397.   Strangely, the visitor felt at home in the foreign land
398.   The political intern arrives in a town barren of people and animals
399.   He decided to live a zero-waste lifestyle for a year
400.   A bomb cyclone hits the city
401.   Rare blue ice appears in the straits of Mackinaw
402.   The top NFL prospect is injured in an accident
403.   He leaves his job of thirty years
404.   Explore a major controversy from opposing perspectives

405.	The baseball coach transfers to an unknown league and takes them to the finals
406.	A graduate works there jobs to pay back her student loans
407.	Declassified papers reveal an assassination attempt
408.	Two elderly men sit on a bench talking about their past while and old black Labrador with a white chin lays between them on the ground
409.	The café is a throwback to another era when people tipped their hats and cowboys roamed the hills
410.	The pregnant waitress gives birth in a diner during a storm
411.	The only visitors he saw this far out were hikers and forestry personnel
412.	A tourist has an affair with a local while traveling in Michigan
413.	She went to Key West to find a new home, but she found ancestral ghosts instead
414.	He is trying to do some kind of puppy mind trick on her
415.	He announces their engagement, but she never agreed
416.	She works without a safety net with hopes of a better tomorrow
417.	She knows a lot about life as a curvy girl, but still doesn't know why it was okay to ridicule someone for how they look
418.	A commuter student who worked two jobs to put his little sister through school
419.	The caregiver on the edge of hope tries one last time
420.	A barista hates the smell and screech of eggnog
421.	The blonde only wants to be accepted for who she is
422.	The dog trainer raises little dogs to find people lost in the woods
423.	She joins a sports league but hasn't played since school
424.	A theater major changes her course of study after one geology dig
425.	The serial killer tells her not to flatter herself
426.	The woman in the pink dress flees the stone building

427.	A daddy's girl falls for an outcast
428.	She knows a lot about being a daughter, but not a mother
429.	His sister is lost in time and she must find her
430.	The girl in the blonde pig tails grows up to be a doctor
431.	She is forced to hide her true self for fear of retribution
432.	He never quite fits in and wants to leave the rinky-dink town
433.	She realizes a coverup surrounding ceiling tiles
434.	A couple on a road trip is mugged and abandoned on the side of the road
435.	He works three jobs to make the rent and security deposit
436.	The remnants of childhood slipped away
437.	He runs away from home to live in the desert
438.	The single dad works at the country store to put his kid through college
439.	The judge asked who she wants to live with: mom or dad
440.	The young girl pretends her home town is going to be attacked by pirates
441.	Her heart cries because she isn't where she thought she should be in life
442.	He survives the dreaded telemarketing vortex of doom
443.	She conjures shapeshifters, dragons, and elves
444.	The substitute teacher teaches her first class
445.	The bookworm wants to live in the novel, but is forced to deal with reality
446.	She is an outcast even among her own family
447.	A country boy is trapped in a rock world
448.	He is always told he was smelly
449.	Someone kills an elf in the North Pole Murder Mystery
450.	Write about Santa's cousin Fredricka
451.	They take a starship to a goldilocks planet and name it Earth 2.0

452.	He is a texting sniper
453.	The midwestern daughter meets a cowboy
454.	Write a new American western
455.	She tempts fate when she says, "Bite me, cupid"
456.	A book detective is lost in a strange world
457.	The anthropologist sees ghosts
458.	Competitive art gallery owners vie for the affections of an artist
459.	He is a fluke of nature, Adonis in human form
460.	After her death, her memories are downloaded into a computer
461.	The legend will not die
462.	Refugees from the stars save humanity
463.	She can run but she can't hide – her past follows her around like a zombie swarm
464.	Make your characters live through the worst thing that could happen
465.	A divine warrior of the sacred waters tries to save an alien race
466.	An ice tsunami crashes like a cross between a train and shattering glass
467.	The continental shelf subverted creating catastrophic tsunamis
468.	I was healthier when the drug dealer lived next door
469.	What if humanity must be mobile again
470.	Time crystals hold a family secret
471.	In her dreams, he confesses he loves her
472.	He thinks she is adorkable
473.	The scientist says the laws of nature are impersonal, but her experience is different
474.	Earth's gravity pulls in another moon
475.	The Dragon Slayer saves the dragon
476.	Her soulmate comes along after she gave up and married another
477.	The wild rose fights the eco terrorist
478.	It is an ancient rite of passage among their people
479.	A plumber finds a map in a book and follows it
480.	She is a scientist at heart and he is an angel fallen to earth to protect her

481.	WWII Eugenics programs never stopped and a military group find the hideout where they plot the next evolution of humankind
482.	Explore punctuated moments of equilibrium of evolution
483.	He only wants a PhD, but then realizes there is life beyond his books
484.	The majority of people regress scientifically except a select few who were excluded from the majority
485.	A dog leaves footprints on his heart
486.	An adventure ends in tragedy
487.	She vanishes from her front yard
488.	Explore the taboo no-go zones of a country
489.	Cadaver dogs in training find an ancient battlefield
490.	A backpacker travels to a foreign town to learn that the place where her mother grew up is now an area of lawlessness
491.	Colleagues visit an entirely robot-run city
492.	An inventor creates a weapon to end all debates
493.	What would he do if faced with a gunman
494.	An exorcism turns into murder
495.	Someone kills a dog walker
496.	The cyber criminal helps the underprivileged
497.	Create a new winter fairy tale
498.	They cross countries in a walk to freedom
499.	She escapes into nature to heal
500.	A woman finds an arsenal under her deceased uncle's bed
501.	Employee fends off three robbers
502.	He sells his boat for $1
503.	A woman sets up her rascal of a big brother with her best friend
504.	An ancient god falls in love with a modern mortal
505.	He is a hitman for god – whatever is needed, he can get it
506.	It is the largest watershed event
507.	She searches for her grandfather's ancestors and finds out she is royalty

508.	An alien transports a group of humans to another planet with evil intentions

509.	She finds an ancient library in the desert

510.	The relic hunter discovers the lost Dutchman mine

511.	A lost tribe follow signs and symbols that show them the way home

512.	While watching a television documentary, a woman sees a painting of herself

513.	Humans from the future send back information necessary to stop a disaster

514.	The doctor falls for his coworker's sister

515.	Power goes out across town in an act of sabotage

516.	Create the next Battle of the Books

517.	There is time enough for love

518.	Life is what happens when you're online

519.	Theirs is a May to remember

520.	He went on a week cruise but found a mystery

521.	The homeowner tries to sell his house, but a scam artist runs a con on renters

522.	Write the story of David and his honor

523.	She has mutant tongue genes

524.	A woman tries to train her dog who won't stop barking

525.	A couple want to return to a simpler life for their family

526.	Write about forgotten possibilities

527.	What does it mean to be human and alive

528.	He wants to engineer sustainable products

529.	A civil war is sparked between Elitist power structures and the populace

530.	A symbologist finds the Original Truth

531.	The English professor found a subglacial lake with a secret

532.	Time travelers return to view the legend of Earth's last days

533.	Write the space adventures of Project Pegasus

534.	She loved vanilla ice cream more than anything

535.	He spends half his life waiting for Google

536.	She's already lived a lifetime with him as her center—and now the amnesiac doesn't remember her

537.	A man from the desert thinks he is a prophet

538.	He wants her to go out with his friend, but she loves him, not his friend

539.	Write about the remnants of childhood through the eyes of a babysitter

540.	She survives the tornado in an office building

541.	Create a coming of age story with a character who longs for more

542.	He tries and tries, but cannot lose weight

543.	Write about the girl who, when attacked by the bully, hits back

544.	She creates borders between her and others that no one could scale until now

545.	The curly-haired girl who lives in a straight-haired world finally accepts herself

546.	After being rejected three times, a man tries one last time to convince her to be his wife

547.	The girl learns kung fu because of the man next door

548.	In the woods beside a flowing stream the camper finds the perfect spot

549.	Love finds a widower and his two children

550.	He keeps secrets for his boss

551.	A reluctant caregiver for his elderly mother needs help

552.	There are friends and then there are real friends who wake in the middle of the night and come to help without asking questions

553.	Three women become roommates while dealing with life, bills, and the occasional romance

554.	The Caretaker: a spy story

555.	Write about rocks and the people who study them

556.	Archaeologists travel the world looking for relics, but find pottery shards more frequently than glittering objects

557.	The unemployed worker takes a fairground job to make it through unemployment

558.	She joins a society of honor students in order to level up her resume, but instead she finds love and a puppy

559.	The historian faces an unexpected truth
560.	The therapist used movies to help people cope
561.	The ruthless killer doesn't have a conscience
562.	Explore self-healing and rapid regeneration
563.	What would their forefathers think about their ideas of freedom
564.	Write about the progression of technology from obsidian blades to computers
565.	The confession is a submission of the heart
566.	Create your own writer's manifesto
567.	She runs away because he breaks her heart
568.	Spider is the turncoat
569.	The ancient god returns to visit his people a hundred years after he left
570.	She walks the beach every day looking for shells
571.	The selkie is the last of her kind
572.	He holds his own against the worst lie ever
573.	The Library Wanderer is a legend among Librarians
574.	He stands outside the fire until he meets her and jumps in
575.	She loves a man who exists only in fiction
576.	In his mind, they've been married for years; in hers, they are divorce
577.	An artefact turns imagined characters into flesh and blood
578.	She departs on a year-long boat voyage
579.	Write the Human's Survival Guide
580.	In the center of everything stands the Tree of Life
581.	She tests video games for a living
582.	Her primary goals after college are to have a baby and get a job
583.	He writes a script for a popular show and travels to sell it
584.	The girl grows up on the shores of Lake Michigan hunting for Petoskey stones
585.	A reluctant guitar player creates magic when strumming the strings
586.	She invents the next revolution in computing technology

587.	In her closet sits three pair of shoes: sneakers for volleyball, flat ballerina slippers, and a pair of 3-inch high kick ass boots in red leather

588.	Write the funeral scene for your main character's hero

589.	She never got punchlines

590.	Write about the ups and downs of unemployment

591.	He disconnects from everything

592.	She tries to dig herself out of a deep depression

593.	He wants to be a Vogue cover model, but never made it

594.	After years on tour, a country singer returns home to Tennessee

595.	The couple move to teach in a foreign land

596.	Write about the trials and triumphs of singledom

597.	She swears to be honest with herself and confronts an ugly truth

598.	Sick of being underestimated, a character vows to never let it happen again

599.	The girl in the red dress finally returns home

600.	She wants to plant something and wanted to watch it grow, but war looms

601.	Write about the fire in his heart

602.	A jock falls in love with a geeky artist

603.	A man afraid of failure uses that fear to fuel his business

604.	She doesn't return his affections

605.	The wayward witch cast a wonky spell

606.	This happens behind closed doors

607.	The doctor must live with his mistakes

608.	Create a comedy about culture clashes

609.	The entrepreneur who reaches for his dreams falls short

610.	A genealogist traces her family to the Greeks and Romans, until she finds a link to a much older civilization

611.	It was the last day of the most amazing person on the planet

612.	She lost everything and has nothing to lose

613.	Create a story around a group of romance writers

614.	On a cold snowy night she finds her true love banging on the door of her cottage
615.	He is happiest when smelling freshly baked bread
616.	She vows to live without regrets
617.	Write about boarders
618.	What if society regresses to a point where we go back to hunting and gathering
619.	He grew up in Ankara, Turkey
620.	The aliens find universal healing qualities in a common earth product
621.	She doesn't want to leave the library because something evil lurks outside
622.	A warrior saves a village under the spell of an evil wizard
623.	She googles Google and breaks the internet
624.	You must not mess with the Grey Wizard
625.	He's so dysfunctional, he breaks himself
626.	She is locked inside a WWII bunker with a spirit sworn to protect it
627.	His arrogance offends her
628.	He creates a pill to mimic the effects of exercise
629.	"I whatever you," he says. "I whatever you more," she answers.
630.	Write about the Belgravia Biblioetheca Sacra
631.	She finds a new haven and brings people there in times of strife when they are hunted
632.	The war hero returning to society must face the demons of her past
633.	He moves to Andover and finds a new affection for blowing things up
634.	She moves to Boston for school, breaks her arm the first day, and falls for the attending physician
635.	The couch potato travels for the first time
636.	For centuries knowledge was passed down, woman to woman, until the chain broke during WWII. Write about the descendant of the woman who finds the information in modern times
637.	The mind plays tricks to put you at ease

About the Author

DARLENE REILLEY is a digital nomad, photographer, and writer. She aims to hit a Venn diagram centering on archaeology, romance, and science fiction. Her goal is to write one hundred epic books that entertain and inspire her readers. When she's not reading, writing, or taking photos, Darlene enjoys cooking, hiking, and snorkeling. Contact Darlene directly through DarWrites.